NELSON'S NEW WEST INDIAN READERS

INFANT BOOK 1

REVISED EDITION

CLIVE BORELY

Illustrated by VAL SANGSTER

Nelson Thornes

Nelson Thornes Ltd
Delta Place
27 Bath Road
CHELTENHAM
GL53 7TH
United Kingdom

© Clive Borely 1972, 1978, 1987

First published 1972
Revised 1978; this edition 1987
Illustrated by Val Sangster

ISBN 978 0 17 566340 8

11 12 / 30 29

Printed by Multivista Global Ltd

TO THE TEACHER

The work in this book can be divided into the following major components:

1 *Sound identification and discrimination.* Children learn the names of the things represented in the pictures and learn to identify the first sounds of the words, e.g. the 'a' sound at the beginning of **apple** and **ant** or the 'b' sound at the beginning of **bat** and **ball**. They will also learn to tell the difference between the sound of 'a' and the sounds of 'e' 'i' 'o', etc. You can test this by getting them to choose, from a number of objects, which one begins with a certain sound.

2 *Association of letters with sounds.* This includes being able to make the sound represented by the letters.

3 *Combining the sounds made by two or more letters into one syllable.* Here children learn to combine 'b' and 'a' to say 'ba' as at the start of **bat** and 'be' as at the start of **bell**. Later they will combine three and four letters to make the appropriate sounds, e.g. **cat, pet, dog,** etc.

4 *Learning a number of sight words by the Look and Say method.* These are commonly used words which do not obey phonic rules and which are needed to make interesting reading before the relevant rules are learnt, e.g. **is, under, over, boy, girl.**

5 *Reading and understanding sentences.* The sentences used are all made up of phonic or sight words learnt in previous lessons. In this way the vocabulary is always familiar to the child; and the stories are based on familiar events which are of interest to children of this age.

Teachers are encouraged to proceed slowly with the early part of the book, ensuring that children can make the appropriate sounds and learn to associate letters and sounds correctly. Constant revision and play activity are necessary, as well as group and individual work. When the class is ready to combine letters into syllables and words, give children time to 'work out' the sounds and help them along. Then try to get them to recognise small combinations as units, e.g. 'ba', 'ca', 'da' as single syllable units and not two separate sounds.

When the child gets to the point of reading sentences the teacher must insist on a natural reading of the whole sentence to convey its meaning. This does not mean that the child cannot pause to work out or remember individual words, but when he has recognised all the words he must be made to re-read the sentence fluently. The teacher should also ask the child appropriate questions where necessary to ensure that he has grasped the meaning of what he has read.

The following are some additional hints on using some of the pages in the text.

Pages 4 and 5 – These pages will take some time. First let the children talk about the pictures with their classmates and then with you. Make sure they call the objects by the right names as indicated on the page. Make sure that all children can pronounce the sound 'a' and then 'e' and can distinguish between them. They are *not expected to read* the words yet.

Page 7 – The pupil is to be taught to combine the initial 'b' sound with the vowel sounds 'a' as in **apple** and 'e' as in **egg**. Be careful to let children say 'be' as in **bell** and not 'be' as in the verb 'to be'. This page will take some time. Help children to work out the combinations rather than make them learn the syllables as in the Look and Say method.

Page 8 – In this lesson the child moves from two letter combinations to three letter combinations. They can do this by learning to add a final consonant sound e.g. **ba** – **bad**, or by learning to put an initial consonant to a combination e.g. **ed** – **bed**. They also learn to put two syllables together. Do not rush this lesson. Go slowly.

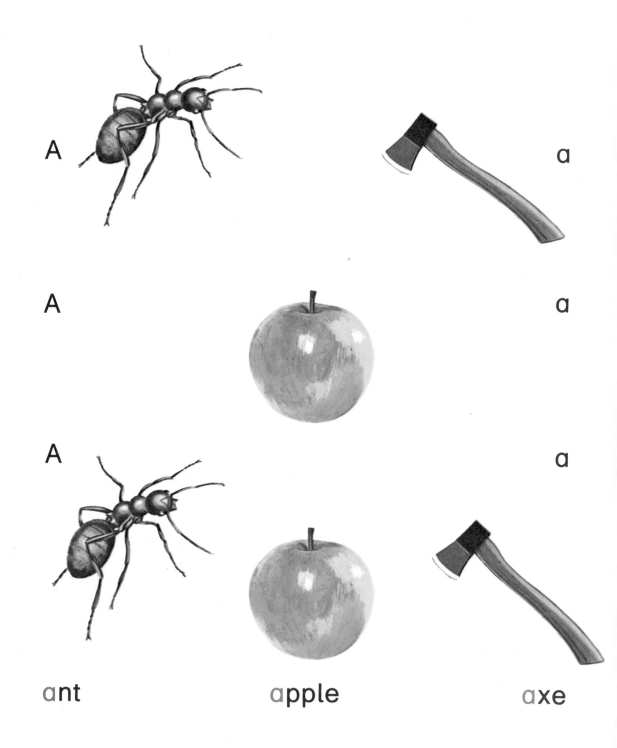

A   a

A   a

A   a

ant   apple   axe

Note to Teacher: See page 3.

4

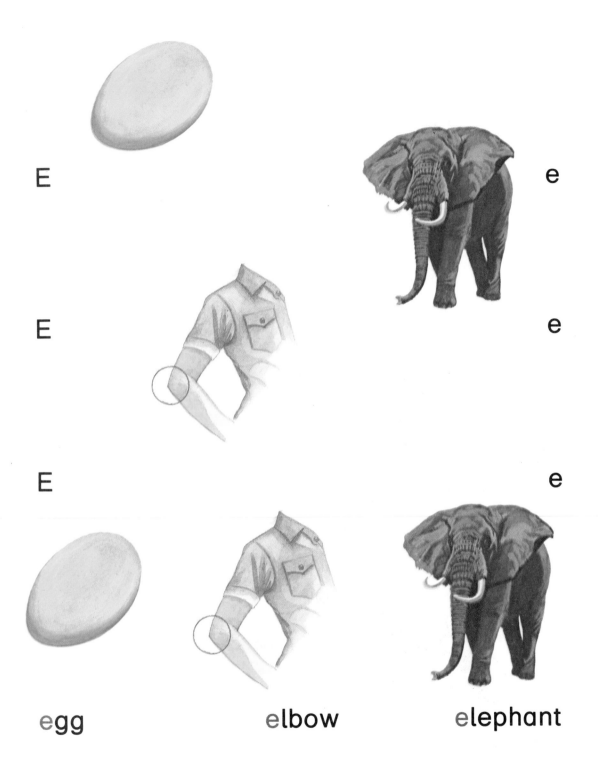

E

e

E

e

E

e

egg

elbow

elephant

Write the first letter sound for each picture.

apple, egg, elephant, axe, ant, elbow

6

B

B

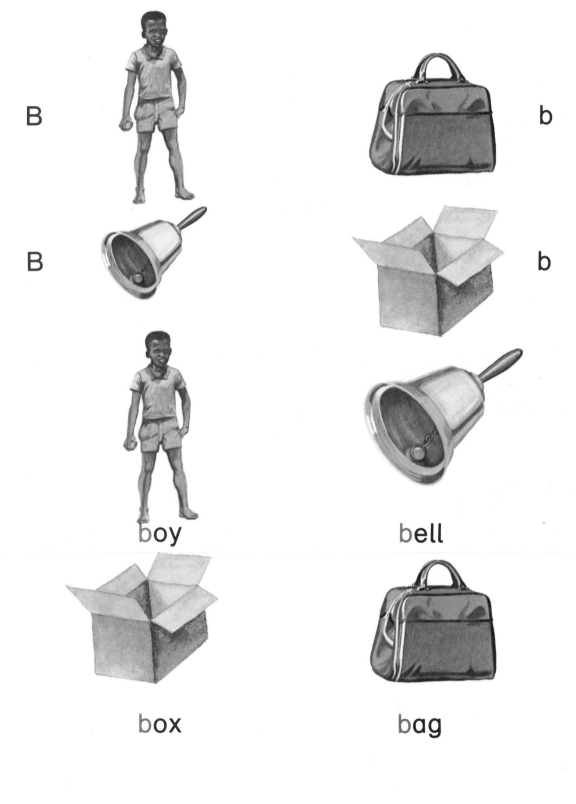

boy

bell

box

bag

ba　be　ab　eb　bab　beb　baba

Note to Teacher: See page 3.

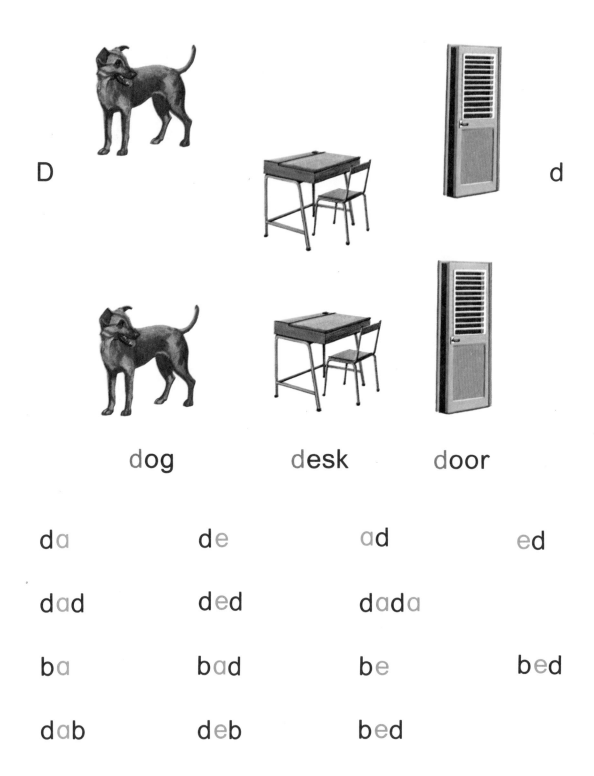

D   d

dog   desk   door

da   de   ad   ed

dad   ded   dada

ba   bad   be   bed

dab   deb   bed

ink

igloo

orange

ox

I	ink	i	I	igloo	i
O	orange	o	O	ox	o

bi	di	bo	do
bib	did	bob	dod
bid	boc	dib	dob
bibi	didi	debi	bobi

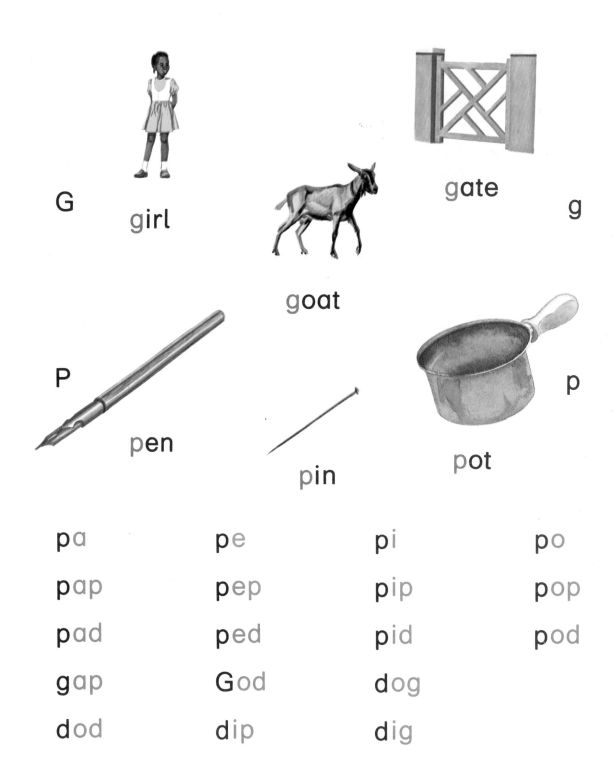

G   girl

goat

gate   g

P   pen

pin

pot   p

pa	pe	pi	po
pap	pep	pip	pop
pad	ped	pid	pod
gap	God	dog	
dod	dip	dig	

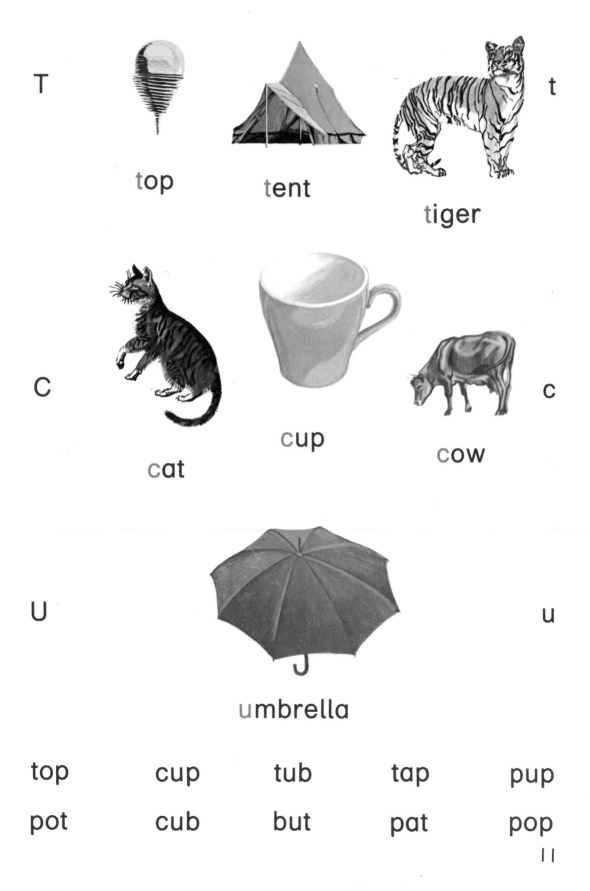

T   t

top   tent   tiger

C   c

cat   cup   cow

U   u

umbrella

| top | cup | tub | tap | pup |
| pot | cub | but | pat | pop |

a	e	i	o	u
bad	bed	bid	bod	bud
cat			cot	cut
cad			cod	cud
pad			pod	
dig			dog	dug
bag	beg	big	bog	bug
tag				tug
bat	bet	bit		but
pat	pet	pit	pot	put
	get		got	gut

Note to Teacher: These two pages contain words that your class should be able to recognise or work out. The words on this page, read from left to right, differ by a change in the vowel. Let the pupils read individually line by line and check that they get their vowel sounds correct.

bad	bag	bat	
bed	beg	bet	
cab	cad	cap	cat
cub	cud	cup	cut
did	dig	dip	
pad	pat		
peg	pet		
pod	pot		
tab	tag		
tub	tug		
God	got		

In the words on this page the change is a final consonant. Check the final consonant sounds as you did for the vowels. If need be, go back to the point where difficult sounds are introduced and ensure that your pupils grasp the letter–sound relationships. (You can make large charts based on these words for class work. Make short sentences with these words for the class to read aloud.)

This is Bob.

He is a boy.

This is Meg.

She is a girl.

This is Peg.

She is a cat.

This is Dob.

He is a dog.

He is big but

   he is not bad.

He is Bob's dog.

This dog has a pup.

This boy has a bat.

Dad has a big pig.

Pat the pup, Dad.

The dog bit the cat.

The cat got a big cut.

Bad dog.

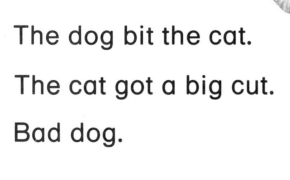

M			m
	man	mango	

leg   lock

L			l

H			h
	hat	house	

mat	met	mop	mug	
lap	leg	lip		
hat	hot	hut	hit	hell
ham	him	hem	hug	hog

Here is Pam.

She is sad.

She has a cut on her leg.

She got a fall on the hill.

Poor Pam!

Here is Pug.

Pug has a pup.

She is Meg's pet dog.

The pup sits on Meg's lap.

Meg has no dolls.

But she is not sad.

She has her pet dog, Pug.

N   n

net   nail

R   r

ring   rope

F   f

fish   flower

fat	fell	fit	fog	fun
rat	red	rid	rod	run
Nat	Ned	nip	nod	nun

man	mat	men	mop
ran	hat	hen	top
Nan	rat	pen	hop
Tim	hut	lap	lad
him	rut	rap	mad
rim	nut	nap	had

Tim can run. Tom can hop.

The cat ran under the bed.

Dad sat in the tub. He had a nap.

The rat ran into Tim's hat.

Tim is mad.

Get the hat, Tim.

The rat hops out.

run	runs	running
hit	hits	hitting
cut	cuts	cutting
dig	digs	digging
get	gets	getting

S   s

snake   soap

sat   set   sit   sob   sun

when   what   where

pin	spin	nap	snap
pill	spill	nag	snag
pot	spot	nip	snip
pat	spat		

Where is the cat?

She is sitting on the mat.

Where is the rat?

He is sitting on the hat.

Where is the dog?

She is with her pup in the tub.

Did you spill ink in the tub?

What is this spot on the cap?

It smells like ham.

A bit of jam fell on my hand.

the	here	all	kind
then	there	ball	find
them	where	fall	mind
this	when	call	hind
that	why	tall	
		wall	
		small	

 Come, Pat, let's play bat and ball.

 I don't mind, but I can't find the ball.

Where is the ball?

 Come, Pat, let's try to find it.

Look, there it is under the tub.

 I have the ball.
You can bat.
Bat this ball.

Boy! You hit the ball hard.
You hit the ball over the wall.
You go and find it.

Can you go over the wall?
I am not so tall.
I will help you over the wall, but you
will have to go and find the ball.

 Come. Stand on this.
Can you see over the wall?
Can you see where it is?

 Yes, I can see it. It fell over there.
It is near the old gate.

 Can you get it?

 No, there is a dog at the gate.
It is a big dog. It looks bad.
We'll have to call.

There is an old man in the hut.

Let's call the old man.
If he is kind, he will get the ball for us.
The old man went to look for the ball.

Here is your ball. Don't hit it so hard.
It will get lost.

Thank you, sir.
I will not hit it so hard again.

Take the ball, Pat.
Let me have the bat. I will bat now.
Okay. Here we go! Bat this if you can.

Tom hits the ball.

Bap! What a hit!
Over the wall again!

We'll have to call the old man.
He will get it for us.
Oh boy, the old man is not there!
Where is he?
He's gone.

Where is the dog?
Is it gone?
No, the dog is there.
Where is the ball?
I can't find the ball.
Look over there. The dog has the ball.
Come here, dog. Come with the ball.

Bow wow! Bow wow!

Come. Come for this bun.
Come to the gate.
Here is the bun.

The dog let the ball go and took the bun.
The ball fell at the gate.

Get the ball, Pat.
Let's play again.

No, it's getting late.
We have to go home.

old	and	hole	the
bold	band	mole	then
cold	hand	role	them
gold	land	pole	this
hold	sand	stole	that
told	stand		

Tom and Pat sit in the sand.
The sun is hot but the sea is cold.
They play in the sand.
Pat digs a big hole.

What are you digging for?
Come and dig.
We may find a bag of gold.

Now the dog digs in the sand.
The sand falls all over Tom and Pat.

 Stop that.
Hold him back.
That sand is cold and wet.

Stop that, you bad dog.
Stop digging the sand.

 Come. Let's go into the sea.
Let's run to the sea.

No, it is too cold. Don't you find it so?

It is cold but I don't mind.

I will play in the sand with the dog.
You go.

But the dog runs into the sea.
Tom and the dog get wet and cold.
Tom runs out and sits in the sun.

I told you it was cold, Pat told Tom.
Go for a run in the sun with the dog.

He plays in the hot sand.
He is not cold now.

The dog is playing in the sea.
Pat calls the dog.

Come here. Come here, you big dog!
Come and play in the sand.

The dog runs to Pat.
He jumps up on Pat.
Now Pat is wet and cold, too.
She is mad.

Get back, you bad dog.

back	deck	sock	luck	Dick
pack	peck	rock	ruck	pick
rack	neck	lock	back	tick
sack	back	mock	duck	sick

over the wall
under the gate
in the tub
on the mat
Look out!
Good luck!
Goodbye!

One cat on a mat,
One rat in a hat,
One dog at a pole near a hole.

"Now how can a rat
Pass that cat on the mat
To get to that hole hear the pole?"

"How how can a rat,"
Thought the rat in the hat,
"Now how can a rat do that?"

"What's that?" said the cat,
As he sat on the mat.
"What's that?" said the cat on the mat.

For the cat on the mat
Saw a hat – just a hat –
Walking past as he sat on the mat.

"Oh, I smell a rat,"
Said the cat on the mat,
"For a hat cannot walk past like that."

So the cat on the mat
Took a spring at the hat,
And the rat ran from under the hat.

"Oho!" said the cat,
Running after the rat,
As he ran to the hole near the pole.

As the cat neared the hole,
The dog shouted, "Hold, hold!"
And the cat ran right back to the mat.

"Thank you, dog! Bye-bye, cat!"
Said the rat in the hat,
As he waved from his hole
Near the pole.

Word List

A	B	C	D	E	F	G	H
am	back	cab	dad	ebb	fad	gap	had
an	bad	cad	dam	egg	fan	God	ham
ant	bag	can	Dad		fat	got	hand
as	band	cap	deck		fed	gull	hat
ask	bat	cat	dell		fall	gun	hell
at	bed	cock	den		fib	gut	hen
	beg	cod	did		fig		hid
	bell	cog	dig		fill		hill
	Ben	cop	dim		fin		hip
	bet	cot	din		fit		hit
	bid	cut	dip		fog		hog
	big	cub	dock		fun		hop
	bill	cup	dog				hot
	bin	cut	doll				hub
	bit		Don				hug
	bog		dot				hull
	buck		duck				hum
	bug		dull				hut
	bun						
	but						

I	J	K	L	M	N	O	P
in	jab	kick	lad	mad	nag	of	pad
ink	jam	kid	lag	man	nap	on	pan
is	jet	kill	land	map	neck		pat
it	jig	king	lap	mat	Ned		peck
	job	kiss	led	Meg	net		peg
	jug	kit	leg	men	nib		pen
	jump		lend	met	Nick		pet
			let	mill	nip		pig
			lid	mit	not		pill
			lip	mock	nun		pit
			lit	mom	nut		pot
			lock	mud			pup
			log	mug			
			lot				
			luck				
			lull				

R	S	T	U	V	W	Y
rag	sack	tab	up	van	wag	yam
ram	sag	tack	under	vat	web	yell
ran	sand	tag		vest	well	yes
rap	sang	tan			wet	yet
rat	sap	tap			wick	
rent	sell	Ted			win	
rest	send	tell			wind	
rib	set	ten			wing	
rig	sick	tick				
rim	sin	till				
ring	sink	Tim				
rip	sip	tin				
rob	sit	tip				
rock	sob	Tom				
rod	song	top				
rot	sop	tot				
rub	sung	tub				
rug	sunk	tuck				
rum		tug				
run						
rut						

bind	bold	hole
find	cold	mole
hind	fold	pole
mind	gold	
	hold	
	told	

than	what
that	when
then	whip
thin	